CW00690877

THE MESSAGE AND PRAYERS OF FATIMA

by
Timothy Tindal-Robertson
and Donal Anthony Foley

*All booklets are published thanks to the
generous support of the members of the
Catholic Truth Society*

CATHOLIC TRUTH SOCIETY
PUBLISHERS TO THE HOLY SEE

Contents

Nihil Obstat: Rev Michael Wheaton
            Diocesan Censor

Imprimatur: ✠ Rt Rev Bishop Mark O'Toole
            Bishop of Plymouth, 15th July 2016

All rights reserved. First published 2016 by The Incorporated Catholic Truth Society, 40-46 Harleyford Road London SE11 5AY Tel: 020 7640 0042 Fax: 020 7640 0046. © 2016 Timothy Tindal-Robertson and Donal Anthony Foley.

ISBN 978 1 78469 139 4

THE CENTENARY OF
OUR LADY OF FATIMA, 1917-2017

The 13th May 2017 is the centenary of Our Lady's first apparition at Fatima. One hundred years later, it is clear that as a result of recent developments with regard to Our Lady's message, it has become more relevant than ever, both for the well-being of the Church today as well as for the development of its mission for the salvation of mankind in the years that lie ahead.

The most important of these developments, in terms of the daily life of members of the Church now and into the future, was the beatification of Francisco and Jacinta by St John Paul II at Fatima, on 13th May 2000, some eighty years after they had died in 1919 and 1920 respectively.

By their beatification, the pope proclaimed that these "two candles whom God lit to illumine humanity", as he described them - aged only nine and seven in 1917 - had been raised up to attain heroic virtue in the ordinary course of their family life, not due to the extraordinary supernatural manifestations with which they were favoured, but because of their fidelity and commitment in fulfilling the requests of Our Lady. When a second permanent miracle of healing is obtained through their intercession, they will then be declared the first child saints in the history of the Church who did not die as martyrs.

Models for Modern Families

Today families who strive to live their vocation with fidelity face challenges never experienced before that have been addressed by Pope Francis in *Amoris Lætitia*. It is at this providential moment that now for the first time ever in her history the Church has raised to the altar the two youngest children of a devout family, as models of sanctification for children and adults alike. Through the inspiring story of how their lives changed after meeting first the angel in 1916 and then Our Lady in 1917, there is traced out an assured path to heaven through life's trials and challenges that can be followed by all under the comforting maternal guidance of Our Lady of Fatima.

After the first apparition on 13th May in 1917, little Jacinta kept on exclaiming enthusiastically, "Oh, what a beautiful Lady", and that night broke her word to keep quiet by telling her parents everything they had seen and heard. "There was something within me that wouldn't let me keep quiet", she tearfully told Francisco and Lucia. That was how the apparition became known, and immediately brought down upon them the suffering which Our Lady had foretold, as the children experienced the doubt, disbelief and opposition of their own parents.

The same effect has been produced throughout salvation history, whenever someone has experienced a true, interior and heartfelt personal encounter with the living God. This is what caused the hearts of Jesus's disciples - and countless others in the ensuing centuries - to "burn within them" (cf. *Lk* 24:32). The divine experience planted in them such unquenchable joy and conviction that it "wouldn't let them keep quiet", and thereafter for the sake of proclaiming the Gospel they were willing to "bear all the sufferings he wills to send you, as an act of reparation for the conversion of sinners" (cf. *Col* 1:24; *2 Tm* 2:12). It was on these terms that Our Lady asked the children, "are you willing to offer yourselves to God?" and when they responded, "Yes", she told them they would have much to suffer, "but the grace of God will be your comfort".

Taking up One's Cross

Conversion, says the *Catechism of the Catholic Church*, is accomplished in daily life by, among other things, accepting suffering and enduring persecution. "Taking up one's cross each day and following Jesus is the surest way of penance" (*CCC* 1435, citing *Lk* 9:23). The lives of Bl. Francisco and Jacinta show that the message of Fatima is the extension to the Church of this Gospel-witnessing experience, in a manner adapted to the circumstances of our times through the mediation of Our Lady and her Immaculate Heart, in order to participate in Jesus's mission: "I came not to call the righteous, but sinners" (*Mk* 2:17).

This indeed is the reason the Church has accepted Our Lady's message: because its "basic content is the truth and the call of the Gospel itself: 'Repent and believe in the Gospel' (*Mk* 1:15). These are the first words that the Messiah addressed to humanity", said the great Pope of the twentieth century, St John Paul II, in his homily at Fatima on 13th May 1982. In his General Audience on 17th May 2000, after beatifying Francisco and Jacinta, the pope described the message of Fatima as "a message of conversion and hope…which is the true Gospel of Christ. Let us receive the light that comes from Fatima, let us be guided by Mary. May her Immaculate Heart be our refuge and the way that leads us to Christ".

Angels "belong to him [Christ]…and are messengers of his saving plan", we are informed by the *Catechism of the Catholic Church* (*CCC* 331). In 1916 an angel appeared to the children and told them that the Hearts of Jesus and Mary had "designs of mercy" upon them, namely, to offer up sacrifices in reparation for sins and the conversion of sinners. "Conversion", wrote St John Paul II, "is the most concrete expression of the working of love and of the presence of mercy in the human world" (*Dives in Misericordia*, n. 6). God's infinite grace and mercy for sinners out of his desire for their conversion and salvation, mediated through the Immaculate Heart of Mary, is the thread running through the apparitions at Fatima, culminating in the vision of the most Holy Trinity experienced by Sr Lucia on 13th June

1929, when she saw Christ crucified and the words "grace and mercy" streaming down from the cross, with Mary present on the altar, offering her Immaculate Heart to the most Holy Trinity. That was the moment, Our Lady told Lucia, when God asked the Holy Father, in union with all the bishops of the world, to consecrate Russia to her Immaculate Heart, "promising to save it by this means". (*Fatima in Lucia's Own Words* - Sr Lucia's memoirs, [hereafter *FILOW*] published by the Postulation Centre at Fatima for the Causes of Canonisation of Bl. Francisco and Jacinta, Vol. I, 18th edition, Nov 2011, p. 198).

The Pardon Prayer which the angel taught the seers comprises the virtues of faith, hope and charity which "are the pledge of the presence and action of the Holy Spirit in the faculties of the human being" (*Compendium of the Catechism of the Catholic Church* 384). The seers repeated this grace-filled prayer for hours on end, and this prepared them for the apparitions of Our Lady in the following year.

The Grace of God

In her first apparition, after Our Lady had told them that the grace of God would comfort them in their suffering for the conversion of sinners, she opened her hands for the first time, and communicated:

a light so intense that as it streamed from her hands, its rays penetrated our hearts and the innermost depths of our souls, making us see ourselves in God who was that light, more clearly than we see ourselves in the best of mirrors. Then, moved by an interior impulse that was also communicated to us, we fell on our knees, repeating in our hearts:

"O most Holy Trinity, I adore you! My God, my God, I love you in the most Blessed Sacrament" (*FILOW*, pp. 175, 176).

After the apparition, Francisco said, "I loved seeing the angel, but I loved still more seeing Our Lady. What I loved most of all was to see Our Lord in that light from Our Lady which penetrated our hearts. I love God so much. But he is very sad because of so many sins."

This profound mystical experience through Our Lady kindled in their hearts that fire of the love of God which did not burn them, so that they were willing to accept whatever suffering he would send for the conversion and salvation of sinners. In the words of Pope Benedict XVI, the Lady "from heaven" was "the teacher who introduced the little seers to a deep knowledge of the love of the Blessed Trinity and led them to savour God himself as the most beautiful reality of human existence" (*Shepherds of Fatima*, CTS, p. 38).

Francisco was absorbed by God the most Holy Trinity, perceived in the light from Our Lady's hands. After the July apparition, he said, "we were on fire in that light which is God and yet we were not burnt. What is God? …we could never put it into words". Jacinta said: "I love Our Lord so much. At times I seem to have a fire in my heart, but it does not burn me".

The Rosary and the Immaculate Heart

Never before in the history of the Church has a revelation of such extraordinary spiritual richness been made through very young children.

Just before Our Lady rose out of sight she urged the seers: "Pray the Rosary every day, in order to obtain peace for the world, and the end of the war". She reiterated this request in each of her six apparitions, and in the last on 13th October she revealed, "I am the Lady of the Rosary".

In the apparition of 13th June, Lucia asked Our Lady to take the enraptured seers to heaven.

> "Yes. I will take Jacinta and Francisco soon. But you are to stay here some time longer. Jesus wishes to make use of you to make me known and loved. He wants to establish in the world devotion to my Immaculate Heart. I promise salvation to those who embrace it, and those souls will be loved by God like flowers placed by me to adorn his throne".

Francisco and Jacinta died aged almost eleven and almost ten on 4th April 1919 and 20th February 1920 respectively, having faithfully borne witness to Our Lady's message through their lives of heroic virtue. Lucia died aged almost

ninety eight on 13th February 2005, after fulfilling her mission, in the letters she wrote to the popes and many people, and through her books.

"Am I to stay here alone", Lucia asked sadly. "No", replied Our Lady. "Don't lose heart. I will never forsake you. My Immaculate Heart will be your refuge and the way that will lead you to God" (*FILOW*, p. 177). These last touching words expressing Mary's maternal consolation form a simple yet deeply meaningful prayer.

The words of Jesus on the cross, "behold your son... behold your mother" (*Jn* 19:26, 27) show that devotion to Mary is his will for us. Jesus wants us to show our love for his Mother and ours, who is filled with his divine graces, and such devotion "corresponds to the objective truth about the Mother of God", as St John Paul II explained in his book, *Crossing the Threshold of Hope* (p. 213). In his General Audience of 7th May 1997, St John Paul II taught that filial devotion to Mary increases our intimacy with Jesus "and leads to the highest levels of perfection" (*Theotokos*, p. 192); for "among creatures no one knows Christ better than Mary, no one can introduce us to a profound knowledge of his mystery better than his Mother" (*Rosarium Virginis Mariae*, n. 14). Accordingly, "the Church's devotion to the Blessed Virgin is an intrinsic element of Christian worship" (Bl. Pope Paul VI, *Marialis Cultus*, n. 56).

Your Will be Done

With regard to the Immaculate Heart of Mary, Pope Benedict XVI said that it resembles the Heart of Christ more than any other, "and for this very reason the liturgy holds them up together for our veneration" (Angelus, 5th June 2005). Earlier, as Cardinal Ratzinger he wrote that "to be devoted to the Immaculate Heart of Mary means to embrace this attitude of heart which makes the *fiat* - 'your will be done' - the defining centre of one's whole life" (*Theological Commentary* on the third part of the secret, in *FILOW*, p. 228).

At the end of this apparition, the children saw the Immaculate Heart of Mary pierced by thorns which encircled it, "outraged by the sins of humanity, and seeking reparation" *(FILOW, p. 177)*.

In the apparition of 13th July, in response to Lucia's request, Our Lady promised that in October she would perform a miracle "for all to see and believe". This was the stupendous miracle of the sun, seen by some seventy thousand people from all over Portugal, and which even unbelievers who had come to mock were obliged to affirm. Then she told them to sacrifice themselves for sinners, and to say many times, especially when they did so: "O Jesus, it is for love of you, for the conversion of sinners, and in reparation for the sins committed against the Immaculate Heart of Mary."

Using this prayer we can offer up as a sacrifice anything that happens in daily life that irritates us or upsets our plans. We are not asked to imitate the extraordinary sacrifices made by the seers, because we have not been favoured with the special role for which they were chosen, but we are asked to follow the example of their heroic acts of penance and self-denial in accordance with our circumstances.

A Vision of Hell

Then follows a very realistic description of hell, which they saw in the light from Our Lady's hands. "The Church affirms the existence of hell and its eternity", but only those go there who at the end of their lives refuse to believe and be converted (*CCC* 1033-1037). Pope Francis wants us to take seriously the existence of the devil and his strategies to tempt us into sin, and has said the devil's greatest achievement has been to make us believe he doesn't exist (cf. *Who is the Devil? What Pope Francis Says*, CTS, 2014).

As the vision ended, Our Lady explained, so kindly and sadly, the particular reason that the seers were shown hell "where the souls of poor sinners go" - because "*to save them* God wishes to establish in the world devotion to my Immaculate Heart" (my emphasis). Here Our Lady is talking about God's plan for saving individuals from the snares of the devil. But then she utters a grave and prophetic pronouncement which directly concerns the history of the Church and the world in our times, in which she speaks of the formidable activities of the "father of lies" (*Jn* 8:44), the prince and deceiver of the whole world (*Jn* 14:30, *Rv* 12:9).

If people did not heed her requests to cease offending God, Our Lady warned that Russia would spread her errors throughout the world, causing wars and persecutions of the Church, the suffering of the Holy Father and the annihilation of various nations. Is this not happening in our time, in the Middle East? Russia's errors, inaugurated by Lenin's Communist Revolution in October 1917, the same month of Our Lady's final apparition at Fatima, involved the attempt to install throughout the world political regimes dedicated to the elimination of God and the Church, which resulted in campaigns of immense destruction and the persecution, slaughter and imprisonment of countless millions.

In our time the unprecedented worldwide campaign of the denial and rejection of God has become more influential than ever, concealed behind various guises such as the culture of death, the dictatorship of relativism denounced by Benedict XVI, materialism, and the "silent apostasy" in European culture of those who live as if God does not exist (*Ecclesia in Europa*, n. 9).

Our Lady then revealed heaven's response to these grave threats to mankind's salvation. It comprised, at the level of the Church, the pope's consecration of Russia to her Immaculate Heart, together with the faithful's first Saturdays communion in reparation to her Immaculate Heart for the blasphemies and ingratitude with which it is pierced by ungrateful men (cf. *Lk* 2:35; *FILOW*, pp. 178, 179, 193-198).

The Five First Saturdays Devotion

St John Paul II fulfilled the first part of this request by his act of consecration of 25th March 1984, which brought about the collapse of the former Soviet Union and the cessation of the persecution of the Church, peacefully, on 25th December 1991, through the intercession of the Immaculate Heart of Mary. I documented this process in my book, *Fatima, Russia and Pope John Paul II*. It was read by the pope in the Polish translation, and he spoke words approving it to the editor, Fr Jan Rokosz, MIC. The miraculous outcome of St John Paul II's act of consecration demonstrated that the unfolding of future events depends on our response to Our Lady's requests, as Our Lady said. This was endorsed by the verdict of Benedict XVI on his pilgrimage to Fatima in May 2010: "we would be mistaken to think that Fatima's prophetic mission is complete" (*Shepherds of Fatima*, p. 41).

The five first Saturdays devotion in reparation to the Immaculate Heart of Mary - the counterpart of the same request that pertains to the faithful - still awaits official approval and implementation by the Church.

At the level of the individual, the devotion to the Immaculate Heart of Mary means fulfilling her requests for prayer, especially daily recitation of the Rosary, penance and sacrifices for the conversion of sinners and in reparation for sins against her Immaculate Heart. It also means imitating her unconditional acceptance of the will of God in our lives.

One would have to read Lucia's memoirs in order to grasp fully the marvellous love of little Jacinta for Jesus and the Immaculate Heart of Mary, and her consequent thirst for suffering which she embraced wholeheartedly, in order to save souls from the torments of hell, the sight of which had affected her deeply. Sr Lucia wrote that this grace flowed from the light they received through the hands of Our Lady in the June apparition, which infused them with a special knowledge and love for the Immaculate Heart of Mary (*FILOW*, p. 127). Here is just one example out of many of the remarkable graces Jacinta received, and which she recounted to Lucia not long before her death.

"You will remain here to make known that God wishes to establish in the world devotion to the Immaculate Heart of Mary... Tell everybody that God grants us graces through the Immaculate Heart of Mary, that people are to ask her for them, and that the Heart of Jesus wants the Immaculate Heart of Mary to be venerated at his side. Tell them also to pray to the Immaculate Heart of Mary for peace since God has entrusted it to her. [St John

Paul II's act of consecration to the Immaculate Heart of Mary brought the Cold War to an end and peace and reunification for East and West Europe]. If I could only put into the hearts of all the fire that is burning within my own heart, and that makes me love the Hearts of Jesus and Mary so very much" (*FILOW*, p. 132).

Teaching us to Pray the Rosary

Next, Our Lady conveyed the urgency of Jesus's thirst on the cross to save souls, when she taught the seers to say this prayer after each mystery of the Rosary:

"O my Jesus, forgive us, save us from the fire of hell. Lead all souls to heaven, especially those who are most in need." (*FILOW*, p. 179).

In August Our Lady urged the seers to "pray very much and make sacrifices for sinners, for many souls go to hell (cf. *Mt* 7:13-14) because there are none to sacrifice themselves and to pray for them" (*FILOW*, p. 180). By this simple offering of sacrifices in the ordinary course of daily life we can help Jesus to save souls. Are we following the example of the seers and doing it?

In the final apparition on 13th October 1917, Our Lady said that she wanted a chapel to be built in her honour, and then, "I am the Lady of the Rosary. Continue always to pray the Rosary every day", as she had urged in each of the previous five apparitions.

18

Finally, looking very sad, Our Lady said: "Do not offend the Lord our God any more, because he is already so much offended."

At this point, while the huge crowd of some seventy thousand people was gazing awestruck at the stupendous miracle of the sun, which appeared to descend to the earth giving out rays of different hues before returning to its place in the sky, the seers saw the Holy Family, with St Joseph and the Child Jesus blessing the world, then Our Lady of Sorrows, and finally Our Lady of Carmel (*FILOW*, pp. 182, 183).

Our Lady of Fatima's Message for the Family

People will be charmed and amazed when the holiness of the little seers, which is scattered throughout the pages of Lucia's memoirs, is gathered together into a coherent story. Here one can only give a brief sample of that treasure yet to be brought out from Fatima's divine reservoir "that you Father have hidden from the wise and understanding and revealed to babes for such was your gracious will" (*Mt* 11:25), to quote from the reading chosen for the Mass of the Beatification of Francisco and Jacinta.

On one occasion, Lucia brought Jacinta a picture of a chalice with a host, such as they actually saw suspended in the air and dripping blood into a chalice underneath in the third apparition of the angel. Radiant with joy, she exclaimed, "It is the hidden Jesus. I love him so much. If only I could receive him in church. Don't they receive Holy Communion in heaven? If they do, then I will go to Holy Communion every day" (*FILOW*, p. 133).

This and so many other marvellous stories of the seers' lives, radiant with the spiritual beauty of innocent children inflamed with the love of God, urgently need to be gathered together and proclaimed as the "Good News" that has not previously been heard in the Church, so that the same love of God and the Church may be infused into today's generation of children, parents and grandparents - the families who form the domestic church, from whom will come the members of the Church in the future.

This gift from heaven to the Church of our time was made possible by the great St John Paul II, the pope endowed with a unique understanding of marriage and the family in God's plan for our salvation, when he decreed, after a special meeting in April 1981 which reversed the previous understanding, that it was possible for children of such a young age to attain heroic virtue.

Help us withstand Pressure of Modern Life

In order to withstand the ever-increasing pressures threatening the Church's teaching on the sacredness of marriage, the family and children, the Church today needs families to strive for that holiness which trustingly embraces the love of God and longing for heaven as the primary purpose and fulfilment of mankind's eternal destiny. Never before in her history has the Church proposed children as the models to lead the way, but there are no mere coincidences in the plans of divine providence, said St John Paul II. God knew these challenging times would come and accordingly sent his Mother to the three shepherd children to show us, through the marvellous working of grace in their lives, the divine mysteries of his kingdom. What we learn through the teaching of the Gospel, the Church and the *Catechism*, these unlettered children were privileged to be taught by Mary Immaculate, face to face, as it were.

Pope Francis has been warning us of the wiles of the enemy (cf. *Who is the Devil?* CTS, 2014), whose errors today threaten to undermine the sacred nature of marriage and the family as ordained by God. It was to warn us about these threats that Our Lady came to Fatima, to provide us with the response from heaven in the message of prayer, penance and reparation for sin that she gave to the shepherd children, who were the youngest to be born of two devout families. In particular, she insisted on daily recitation of the Rosary, knowing that "this very fruitful way of praying is not only efficacious in warding off evils and preventing calamities, but is also of great help in fostering Christian life... If evils increase, the devotion of the People of God should also increase" (Bl. Pope Paul VI, *Christi Matri*, September 1966). In his Apostolic Letter on the Rosary, St John Paul II taught that its mysteries "put us in living communion with Jesus through - we might say - the heart of his Mother" and constitute an effective support for the family, "the primary cell of society, increasingly menaced by forces of disintegration" (*Rosarium Virginis Mariae*, nn. 2, 6).

The Divine Message of Fatima

The Blessed Virgin's divine message at Fatima issued from her Immaculate Heart - the only one in the Church whom the devil is completely unable to influence with all his insidious strategies for our undoing. This is why we need to have recourse to her, in order to overcome the world, the sins of the flesh and the malicious scheming of the devil, by complying with her simple requests. It was their fidelity and commitment in responding to her requests, said St John Paul II, and not the exceptional supernatural manifestations with which they were favoured, which gained for Blessed Francisco and Jacinta the Church's highest honour of the altar. In order to successfully confront the enemy, and advance the New Evangelisation, and ensure the salvation of our souls and those of our families, let us follow their example and entrust ourselves to Our Lady and the message she gave us at Fatima. The lives of the first child saints in the history of the Church demonstrate that one hundred years later, this message is more relevant than ever.

Fatima Prayers and Devotions

Morning Offering

O my God, in union with the Immaculate Heart of Mary (*here kiss your brown scapular as a sign of your consecration - this carries a partial indulgence*), I offer you the precious blood of Jesus from all the altars throughout the world, joining with it the offering of my every thought, word and action of this day.

O my Jesus, I desire today to gain every indulgence and merit I can, and I offer them together with myself, to Mary Immaculate, that she may best apply them to the interests of thy most Sacred Heart.

Precious Blood of Jesus, *save us*

Sorrowful and Immaculate Heart of Mary, *pray for us*

Sacred Heart of Jesus, *have mercy on us.*

Pardon Prayer

My God, I believe, I adore, I hope and I love you. I ask pardon of you for those who do not believe, do not adore, do not hope and do not love you.

Angel's Reparation Prayer

Most Holy Trinity, Father, Son and Holy Spirit, I adore you profoundly and I offer you the most precious body, blood, soul and divinity of Jesus Christ, present in all the tabernacles of the world, in reparation for the outrages, sacrileges and indifference with which he himself is offended. And through the infinite merits of his most Sacred Heart and the Immaculate Heart of Mary, I beg of you the conversion of poor sinners.

Decade Prayer

O my Jesus, forgive us our sins, save us from the fires of hell. Lead all souls to heaven, especially those most in need of thy mercy.

Eucharistic Prayer

O most Holy Trinity, I adore you. My God, my God, I love you in the most Blessed Sacrament.

Sacrifice Prayer

O Jesus, it is for love of you, for the conversion of sinners, and in reparation for the sins committed against the Immaculate Heart of Mary.

Prayer for the Canonisation of Blessed Jacinta and Francisco Marto

Most Holy Trinity, Father, Son and Holy Spirit, I adore you profoundly and I thank you for the apparitions of the most Holy Virgin in Fatima.

By the infinite merits of the Sacred Heart of Jesus and through the intercession of the Immaculate Heart of Mary I implore you - if it should be for your greater glory and the good of our souls - to glorify in the sight of your Holy Church Blessed Francisco and Jacinta, granting us through their intercession the grace which we implore. Amen.

Our Father, Hail Mary, Glory be…

Please send details of any favours received through the intercession of Blessed Francisco and Jacinta to: Secretariado dos Pastorinhos, Apartado 6, P-2496-908 Fatima, Portugal. secretariado@pastorinhos.com

Prayer for the Beatification of the Servant of God Sr Lucia

Most Holy Trinity, Father, Son and Holy Spirit, I adore you profoundly and I thank you for the apparitions of the Blessed Virgin Mary in Fatima that revealed to the world the riches of her Immaculate Heart. By the infinite merits of the Sacred Heart of Jesus and through the intercession of the Immaculate Heart of Mary, I implore you, if it should be for your greater glory and the good of our souls, to glorify Sr Lucia, one of the Shepherds of Fatima, by granting us the grace which we implore through her intercession. Amen.

Our Father, Hail Mary, Glory be…

Please send details of any favours received though Sr Lucia's intercession to: Carmelo de Santa Teresa, Rua de Santa Teresa, no 16, 3000-359, Coimbra, Portugal. causabeatificacaolucia@lucia.pt

Our Lady of Fatima
and the Rosary

At every one of her six Fatima apparitions between May and October 1917, Our Lady specifically asked for the Rosary to be said. This aspect of her message could not have been more emphatic.

On 13th May 1917, she said: "Pray the Rosary every day to obtain peace for the world and an end to the war."

On 13th June: "I want you to pray the Rosary every day."

On 13th July: "I want you to continue to pray the Rosary every day in honour of Our Lady of the Rosary, to obtain peace for the world and the end of the war because only she can help you."

On 19th August: "Continue praying the Rosary every day."

On 13th September: "Continue to pray the Rosary every day in order to obtain the end of the war."

And on 13th October: "I am the Lady of the Rosary. Continue always to pray the Rosary every day."

Rosary Meditations Based on the
New Testament and the Fatima Message

The Joyful Mysteries

The Annunciation

In the sixth month the angel Gabriel was sent by God to a town in Galilee called Nazareth, to a virgin betrothed to a man named Joseph, of the House of David; and the virgin's name was Mary. He went in and said to her, "Rejoice, so highly favoured, the Lord is with you." (*Lk* 1:26-28)

"I have come to ask you to come here for six months in succession, on the 13th day, at this same hour. Later on, I will tell you who I am and what I want. Afterwards, I will return here yet a seventh time." (Our Lady to the children, 13th May 1917, *FILOW*)

The Visitation

Mary set out at that time and went as quickly as she could to a town in the hill country of Judah. She went into Zechariah's house and greeted Elizabeth. Now as soon as Elizabeth heard Mary's greeting, the child leapt in her womb and Elizabeth was filled with the Holy Spirit. (*Lk* 1:39-41)

This meeting of Our Lady and her cousin St Elizabeth shows us Mary's great faith and deep humility. And thinking always of God's mercy, Mary answers her cousin:

"My soul magnifies the Lord and my spirit rejoices in God my Saviour, for he has regarded the low estate of his handmaiden" (*Lk* 1:46-48). The Virgin Mary and St Elizabeth intone here the most beautiful canticle of praise to God. Their lips are moved by the Holy Spirit. But, after all, was not Mary the living temple of the adorable Trinity? (*Calls from the Message of Fatima* by Sr Lucia)

The Nativity

So Joseph set out from the town of Nazareth in Galilee and travelled up to Judaea, to the town of David called Bethlehem, since he was of David's House and line, in order to be registered together with Mary, his betrothed, who was with child. (*Lk* 2:4-5)

In the third decade of the Rosary, we recall the birth of Jesus Christ, God made man. He is the masterpiece of love, God who comes down from heaven to earth to save his poor creatures. He came into the world as a man and manifested himself as Light, Light which shines in the darkness: present among us today as then, but his humanity is veiled. He is present in his word and in his works, in the Eucharist and in the Sacraments of the Church and in the person of each of our brothers and sisters. (*Calls from the Message of Fatima*)

The Presentation in the Temple

And when the day came for them to be purified as laid down by the Law of Moses, they took him up to Jerusalem to present him to the Lord. (*Lk* 2:22)

"O Lord, make me a saint. Keep my heart always pure, for you alone." Then it seemed that in the depths of my heart, our dear Lord distinctly spoke these words to me: "The grace granted to you this day will remain living in your soul, producing fruits of eternal life." (On the occasion of Lucia's first Holy Communion, *FILOW* p. 73)

The Finding of the Child Jesus in the Temple

Every year his parents used to go to Jerusalem for the feast of the Passover. When he was twelve years old, they went up for the feast as usual. When they were on their way home after the feast, the boy Jesus stayed behind in Jerusalem without his parents knowing it…They were overcome when they saw him, and his mother said to him, "My child, why have you done this to us? See how worried your father and I have been, looking for you." "Why were you looking for me?" he replied. "Did you not know that I must be busy with my Father's affairs?" (*Lk* 2:41-42; 48-49)

"Are you willing to offer yourselves to God to bear all the sufferings he wills to send you, as an act of reparation for the sins by which he is offended, and of supplication for the conversion of sinners?"

"Yes, we are willing," was our reply.

"Then, you are going to have much to suffer, but the grace of God will be your comfort." (Our Lady to the children, 13th May 1917, *FILOW* p. 175)

The Mysteries of Light

The Baptism in the Jordan

As soon as Jesus was baptised he came up from the water, and suddenly the heavens opened and he saw the Spirit of God descending like a dove and coming down on him. And a voice spoke from heaven, "This is my Son, the Beloved; my favour rests on him." (*Mt* 3:16-17)

Suddenly the whole chapel was illumined by a supernatural light, and above the altar appeared a cross of light, reaching to the ceiling. In a brighter light on the upper part of the cross, could be seen the face of a man and his body as far as the waist, upon his breast was a dove also of light and nailed to the cross was the body of another man. (Sr Lucia's vision of the Trinity, 13th June 1929, *FILOW* p. 197)

The Wedding at Cana

The mother of Jesus said to him, "They have no wine." Jesus said "Woman, why turn to me? My hour has not come yet." His mother said to the servants, "Do whatever he tells you." (*Jn* 2:3-5)

"You have seen hell where the souls of poor sinners go. To save them, God wishes to establish in the world devotion to my Immaculate Heart. If what I say to you is done, many souls will be saved and there will be peace." (Our Lady to the children, 13th July 1917 *FILOW* p. 210)

The Proclamation of the Kingdom of God

After John had been arrested, Jesus went into Galilee. There he proclaimed the Good News from God. "The time has come," he said "and the kingdom of God is close at hand. Repent, and believe the Good News." (*Mk* 1:14-15)

"The insistent invitation of Mary most Holy to penance is nothing but the manifestation of her maternal concern for the fate of the human family, in need of conversion and forgiveness." (Pope John Paul II, Message for the 1997 World Day of the Sick)

The Transfiguration

He took with him Peter and John and James and went up the mountain to pray. As he prayed, the aspect of his face was changed and his clothing became brilliant as lightning. (*Lk* 9:28-29)

"We beheld a Lady all dressed in white. She was more brilliant than the sun, and radiated a light more clear and intense than a crystal glass filled with sparkling water, when the rays of the burning sun shine through it." (Sr

Lucia describing Our Lady's appearance on 13th May 1917, *FILOW* p. 174)

The Institution of the Eucharist

When evening came he was at table with the twelve disciples. Now as they were eating, Jesus took some bread, and when he had said the blessing he broke it and gave it to the disciples. "Take it and eat;" he said "this is my body." Then he took a cup, and when he had returned thanks he gave it to them. "Drink all of you from this," he said "for this is my blood, the blood of the covenant, which is to be poured out for many for the forgiveness of sins." (*Mt* 26:20; 26-28)

I brought Jacinta a picture of a chalice with a host. She took it, kissed it, and radiant with joy she exclaimed: "It is the hidden Jesus, I love him so much, If only I could receive him in church. Don't they receive Holy Communion in heaven? If they do, then I will go to Holy Communion every day." (Jacinta, while ill, speaking to Lucia, *FILOW* p. 133)

The Sorrowful Mysteries

The Agony in the Garden

They came to a small estate called Gethsemane, and Jesus said to his disciples, "Stay here while I pray." Then he took Peter and James and John with him. And a sudden fear came over him, and great distress. And he said to them,

"My soul is sorrowful to the point of death. Wait here, and keep awake." (*Mk* 14:32-35)

"Here as in the other events of his life, Jesus Christ is for us a model, which we must follow and seek to imitate. Although he was God and had, therefore, all grace and strength, he was also truly human; and he chose to prepare himself by prayer, to submit his human will to that of the Father, who needed him as an expiatory victim for the sins of humanity." (*Calls from the Message of Fatima*)

The Scourging at the Pillar

Then he released Barabbas for them. He ordered Jesus to be first scourged and then handed over to be crucified. (*Mt* 27:26)

"I've such pains in my chest, but I don't say anything. I'm suffering for the conversion of sinners…. I'll suffer for love of Our Lord, to make reparation to the Immaculate Heart of Mary, for the conversion of sinners and for the Holy Father." (Jacinta to Lucia, *FILOW*, p. 59; p. 60)

The Crowning with Thorns

Then they stripped him and made him wear a scarlet cloak, and having twisted some thorns into a crown they put this on his head and placed a reed in his right hand. To make fun of him they knelt to him saying, "Hail, king of the Jews." (*Mt* 27:28-29)

The evening before she fell sick, Jacinta said: "I've a terrible headache and I'm so thirsty. But I won't take a drink, because I want to suffer for sinners."

On another occasion I noticed, as we left the house, that Francisco was walking very slowly:

"What's the matter?" I asked him. "You seem unable to walk!"

"I've such a bad headache, and I feel as though I'm going to fall."

"Then don't come. Stay at home."

"I don't want to. I'd rather stay in the church with the hidden Jesus". (*FILOW*, p. 161)

The Carrying of the Cross

They then took charge of Jesus, and carrying his own cross he went out of the city to the place of the skull or, as it was called in Hebrew, Golgotha. (*Jn* 19:17)

The Crucifixion and Death of Our Lord

When they reached the place called The Skull, they crucified him there and the two criminals also, one on the right, the other on the left. Jesus said, "Father, forgive them; they do not know what they are doing." (*Lk* 23:33-34)

"You at least try to console me and say that I promise to assist at the hour of death, with the graces necessary for salvation, all those who, on the first Saturday of five consecutive months, shall confess, receive Holy

Communion, recite five decades of the Rosary, and keep me company for fifteen minutes while meditating on the fifteen mysteries of the Rosary, with the intention of making reparation to me." (Our Lady to Sr Lucia, 10th December 1925, *FILOW*, p. 194)

The Glorious Mysteries

The Resurrection

The angel spoke; and he said to the women, "There is no need for you to be afraid. I know you are looking for Jesus, who was crucified. He is not here, for he has risen, as he said he would. Come and see the place where he lay, then go quickly and tell his disciples." (*Mt* 28:5-7)

"I will take Jacinta and Francisco [to heaven] shortly; but you will stay here for some time to come. Jesus wants to use you to make me known and loved. He wishes to establish the devotion to my Immaculate Heart throughout the world. I promise salvation to whoever embraces it; these souls will be dear to God, like flowers put by me to adorn his throne." (Our Lady to the children, 13th June 1917, *FILOW*, p. 194)

The Ascension of Christ into Heaven

He was lifted up while they looked on, and a cloud took him from their sight. (*Ac* 1:9)

Then Our Lady began to rise serenely, going up towards the east, until she disappeared in the immensity of space. The light that surrounded her seemed to open up a path before her in the firmament. (Our Lady's return to heaven, 13th May 1917, *FILOW*, p. 176)

The Descent of the Holy Spirit

When Pentecost day came round, they had all met in one room, when suddenly they heard what sounded like a powerful wind from heaven, the noise of which filled the entire house in which they were sitting; and something appeared to them that seemed like tongues of fire; these separated and came to rest on the head of each of them. (*Ac* 2:1-4)

One day during Jacinta's illness, she told Lucia: "I so like to tell Jesus that I love him. Many times, when I say it to him, I seem to have a fire in my heart, but it doesn't burn me." Another time she said: "I love Our Lord and Our Lady so much, that I never get tired of telling them that I love them." (Jacinta speaking to Lucia, *FILOW*, p. 56)

The Assumption

Those who have died in Christ will be the first to rise, and then those of us who are still alive will be taken up in the clouds, together with them; to meet the Lord in the air. So we shall stay with the Lord for ever. With such thoughts as these you should comfort one another. (1 *Th* 4:17-18)

One day Lucia asked Jacinta: "What are you going to do in heaven?" She replied: "I'm going to love Jesus very much, and the Immaculate Heart of Mary, too. I'm going to pray a lot for you, for sinners, for the Holy Father, for my parents and my brothers and sisters, and for all the people who have asked me to pray for them…" (*FILOW*, p. 62)

*The Coronation of Our Lady in Heaven
and the Glory of the Saints*

Now a great sign appeared in heaven: a woman, adorned with the sun, standing on the moon, and with the twelve stars on her head for a crown. (*Rv* 12:1)

"When you pray the Rosary, say after each mystery: 'O my Jesus, forgive us, save us from the fire of hell. Lead all souls to heaven, especially those who are most in need.'" (Decade Prayer, *FILOW*, p. 179)

"I am the Lady of the Rosary. Continue always to pray the Rosary every day…. Do not offend the Lord our God any more, because he is already so much offended." (Our Lady's last words, 13th October 1917, *FILOW*, p. 182)

ACTS OF CONSECRATION
AND REPARATION

Consecration to the Immaculate Heart of Mary

Virgin Mary, Mother of God and our Mother, to your Immaculate Heart we consecrate ourselves, in an act of total entrustment to the Lord. By you we will be led to Christ. By him and with him we will be led to the Father. We will walk in the light of faith, and we will do everything so that the world may believe that Jesus Christ is the one sent by the Father. With him we wish to carry his love and salvation to the ends of the earth. Under the protection of your Immaculate Heart, we will be one people with Christ. We will be witnesses of his Resurrection. By him we will be led to the Father, for the glory of the most Holy Trinity, whom we adore, praise and bless forever. Amen.

A Solemn Act of Consecration to the
Immaculate Heart of Mary by Pope Pius XII

Most Holy Virgin Mary, tender Mother of men, to fulfil the desires of the Sacred Heart of Jesus and the request of the Vicar of your Son on earth, we consecrate ourselves and our families to your Sorrowful and Immaculate Heart, O Queen of the most Holy Rosary, and we recommend to you all the people of our country and all the world.

Please accept our consecration, dearest Mother, and use us as you wish to accomplish your designs in the world.

O Sorrowful and Immaculate Heart of Mary, Queen of the most Holy Rosary, and Queen of the World, rule over us, together with the Sacred Heart of Jesus Christ, our King. Save us from the spreading flood of modern paganism; kindle in our hearts and homes the love of purity, the practice of a virtuous life, an ardent zeal for souls, and a desire to pray the Rosary more faithfully.

We come with confidence to you, O Throne of Grace and Mother of Fair Love. Inflame us with the same divine fire which has inflamed your own Sorrowful and Immaculate Heart. Make our hearts and homes your shrine, and through us make the Heart of Jesus, together with your rule, triumph in every heart and home. Amen.

Venerable Pope Pius XII as at: *https://www.ewtn.com/Devotionals/heart/Im_consecr.htm*

Act of Consecration of Modern World to Our Lady of Fatima made by Pope John Paul II at Fatima on 13th May 1982

1. "We have recourse to your protection, holy Mother of God."

As I utter the words of this antiphon with which the Church of Christ has prayed for centuries, I find myself today in this place chosen by you, O Mother, and by you particularly loved.

I am here, united with all the Pastors of the Church in that particular bond whereby we constitute a body and a college, just as Christ desired the apostles to be in union with Peter.

In the bond of this union, I utter the words of the present Act, in which I wish to include, once more, the hopes and anxieties of the Church in the modern world.

Forty years ago and again ten years later, your servant Pope Pius XII, having before his eyes the painful experience of the human family, entrusted and consecrated to your Immaculate Heart the whole world, especially the peoples for which you had particular love and solicitude.

This world of individuals and nations I too have before my eyes today, as I renew the entrusting and consecration carried out by my Predecessor in the See of Peter: the world of the second millennium that is drawing to a close, the modern world, our world today.

The Church, mindful of the Lord's words: "Go… and make disciples of all nations…and lo, I am with you always, to the close of the age" (*Mt* 28:19-20), renewed, at the Second Vatican Council, her awareness of her mission in this world.

And therefore, O Mother of individuals and peoples, you who "know all their sufferings and their hopes", you who have a mother's awareness of all the struggles between good and evil, between light and darkness, which afflict the modern world, accept the cry which we, as though moved by the Holy Spirit, address directly to your Heart. Embrace, with the love of the Mother and Handmaid, this human world of ours, which we entrust and consecrate to you, for we are full of disquiet for the earthly and eternal destiny of individuals and peoples.

In a special way we entrust and consecrate to you those individuals and nations which particularly need to be entrusted and consecrated.

We have recourse to your protection, holy Mother of God: reject not the prayers we send up to you in our necessities.

Reject them not.

Accept our humble trust and our act of entrusting.

2. "For God so loved the world that he gave his only Son, that whoever believes in him should not perish but have eternal life" (*Jn* 3:16).

It was precisely by reason of this love that the Son of God consecrated himself for all mankind: "And for their sake I consecrate myself, that they also may be consecrated in truth" (*Jn* 17:19).

By reason of that consecration the disciples of all ages are called to spend themselves for the salvation of the world, and to supplement Christ's afflictions for the sake of his body, that is the Church (cf. 2 *Co* 12:15; *Col* 1:24).

Before you, Mother of Christ, before your Immaculate Heart, I today, together with the whole Church, unite myself with our Redeemer in this his consecration for the world and for people, which only in his divine Heart has the power to obtain pardon and to secure reparation.

The power of this consecration lasts for all time and embraces all individuals, peoples and nations. It overcomes every evil that the spirit of darkness is able to awaken, and has in fact awakened in our times, in the heart of man and in his history.

The Church, the Mystical Body of Christ, unites herself, through the service of Peter's successor, to this consecration by our Redeemer.

Oh, how deeply we feel the need for consecration on the part of humanity and of the world - our modern world - in union with Christ himself. The redeeming work of Christ, in fact, must be shared in by the world by means of the Church.

Oh, how pained we are by all the things in the Church and in each one of us that are opposed to holiness and consecration. How pained we are that the invitation to repentance, to conversion, to prayer, has not met with the acceptance that it should have received.

How pained we are that many share so coldly in Christ's work of Redemption. That "what is lacking in Christ's afflictions" is so insufficiently completed in our flesh.

And so, blessed be all those souls that obey the call of eternal Love. Blessed be all those who, day after day, with undiminished generosity accept your invitation, O Mother, to do what your Jesus tells them (cf. *Jn* 2:5) and give the

Church and the world a serene testimony of lives inspired by the gospel.

Above all blessed be you, the Handmaid of the Lord, who in the fullest way obey the divine call.

Hail to you, who are wholly united to the redeeming consecration of your Son.

Mother of the Church, enlighten the People of God along the paths of faith, of hope and love. Help us to live with the whole truth of the consecration of Christ for the entire human family of the modern world.

3. In entrusting to you, O Mother, the world, all individuals and peoples, we also entrust to you the consecration itself, for the world's sake, placing it in your motherly Heart.

Oh, Immaculate Heart, help us to conquer the menace of evil, which so easily takes root in the hearts of the people of today, and whose immeasurable effects already weigh down upon our modern world and seem to block the paths towards the future.

From famine and war, deliver us.

From nuclear war, from incalculable self-destruction, from every kind of war, deliver us.

From sins against the life of man from its very beginning, deliver us.

From hatred and from the demeaning of the dignity of the children of God, deliver us.

From every kind of injustice in the life of society, both national and international, deliver us.

From readiness to trample on the commandments of God, deliver us.

From attempts to stifle in human hearts the very truth of God, deliver us.

From sins against the Holy Spirit, deliver us, deliver us.

Accept, O Mother of Christ, this cry laden with the sufferings of all individual human beings, laden with the sufferings of whole societies.

Let there be revealed, once more, in the history of the world your infinite power of merciful Love. May it put a stop to evil. May it transform consciences. May your Immaculate Heart reveal for all the light of hope.

Taken from *L'Osservatore Romano*, Weekly Edition in English, 24th May 1982 at *http://www.ewtn.com/library/PAPALDOC/JPCONFAT.htm*

Act of Reparation to the Immaculate Heart of Mary

Holy Virgin Mary, our dear Mother, in showing us your heart encircled with thorns, symbols of the blasphemies and ingratitude with which men, ungrateful men, repay the tenderness of your love, you asked us to console you and make reparation.

Therefore we humbly approach to make reparation to your Immaculate Heart, and in a special way to atone for the indignities directed towards your Immaculate Conception and holy virginity.

There are many who deny that you are the Mother of God, and will not accept you as the tender Mother of men. Others pour out upon your sacred images their uncontrolled hate, or seek to instil in men's hearts, especially in the hearts of innocent children, indifference and contempt towards you.

Most Holy Virgin, we wish to show the sorrow we feel because of these offences, and we promise to make reparation with our sacrifices, Holy Communions and prayers for the sins of your ungrateful children. Recognising that we ourselves do not always honour and love you as we should, we humbly ask your merciful forgiveness.

OTHER MARIAN PRAYERS

The Angelus

V. The angel of the Lord declared unto Mary,

R. *And she conceived of the Holy Spirit.*

Hail Mary…

V. Behold the handmaid of the Lord.

R. *Be it done to me according to thy word.*

Hail Mary…

V. And the word was made flesh,

R. *And dwelt among us.*

Hail Mary…

V. Pray for us O holy Mother of God,

R. *That we may be made worthy of the promises of Christ.*

Let us pray:

Pour forth, we beseech thee O Lord, thy grace into our hearts that we to whom the incarnation of Christ, thy Son, was made known by the message of an angel, may by his Passion and Cross be brought to the glory of his Resurrection: through the same Christ, Our Lord.

R. *Amen.*

The Regina Caeli - Queen of Heaven

V. O Queen of Heaven, rejoice, alleluia.

R. *For he whom you did merit to bear, alleluia.*

V. Has risen, as he said, alleluia.

R. *Pray for us to God, alleluia.*

V. Rejoice and be glad, O Virgin Mary, alleluia.

R. *For the Lord has truly risen, alleluia.*

Let us pray:

O God, who gave joy to the world through the Resurrection of thy Son, Our Lord Jesus Christ, grant, we beseech thee, that through the intercession of the Virgin Mary, his Mother, we may obtain the joys of everlasting life: through the same Christ Our Lord.

R. *Amen.*

Memorare

Remember, O most gracious Virgin Mary, that never was it known that anyone who fled to thy protection, implored thy help, or sought thine intercession was left unaided.

Inspired by this confidence, I fly unto thee, O Virgin of virgins, my Mother; to thee do I come, before thee I stand, sinful and sorrowful. O Mother of the Word Incarnate, despise not my petitions, but in thy mercy hear and answer me. Amen.

Magnificat

My soul glorifies the Lord, my spirit rejoices in God my saviour. He looks on his servant in her lowliness; henceforth all generations will call me blessed. The Almighty works marvels for me, holy his name. His mercy is from age to age, on those who fear him. He puts forth his arm in strength and scatters the proud hearted. He casts the mighty from their thrones and raises the lowly. He fills the starving with good things, sends the rich away empty. He protects Israel, his servant, remembering his mercy, the mercy promised to our fathers, to Abraham and his sons for ever. Amen.

NOVENAS TO OUR LADY OF FATIMA

Nine Day Short Novena to Our Lady of Fatima

Most Holy Virgin, who has deigned to come to Fatima to reveal to the three little shepherds the treasures of graces hidden in the recitation of the Rosary, inspire our hearts with a sincere love of this devotion, so that by meditating on the mysteries of our redemption that are recalled in it, we may gather the fruits and obtain the conversion of sinners, the conversion of Russia, and this favour that I so earnestly seek…which I ask of you in this novena, for the greater glory of God, for your own honour, and for the good of all people. Amen

Our Father, Hail Mary, Glory be…

Nine Day Longer Novena to Our Lady of Fatima

Day 1

Our Lady of the Rosary, the Holy Trinity sent the Angel of Peace to the three shepherd children, Jacinta, Lucia and Francisco, to prepare them for their meetings with you. Take away our fears and by your intercession give us the grace to believe, hope, adore and love God, and also to ask pardon of those who do not believe, nor adore, nor hope, nor love him. May we pray thus, confident that your Immaculate Heart, and the Sacred Heart of Jesus, your Son, are always ready to listen to our prayers.

Now make your petition to Our Lady of Fatima
Our Father, Hail Mary, Glory be…

Day 2

Our Lady of the Rosary, just as the Angel of Peace urged the children to pray fervently because your Immaculate Heart, and the Sacred Heart of Jesus, had merciful designs on them, so also may we have the grace through your intercession to offer our prayers and sacrifices to God, the Most High, so that everything we do may become an act of reparation for the sins by which he is offended, and in supplication for sinners. By doing this, particularly through praying the Rosary, may we help to bring peace to the world, while bearing and accepting with patience the sufferings of life.

Now make your petition to Our Lady of Fatima
Our Father, Hail Mary, Glory be…

Day 3

Our Lady of the Rosary, just as the Angel of Peace knelt down before the precious body and blood of your divine Son, and prayed a profound prayer of adoration and reparation for all the sins of mankind, may we too offer prayers of adoration and reparation to God, and partake worthily of Holy Communion; and through the infinite merits of his most Sacred Heart, and your Immaculate Heart, may we earnestly pray for the conversion of sinners.

Now make your petition to Our Lady of Fatima
Our Father, Hail Mary, Glory be…

Day 4

Our Lady of the Rosary, you came from heaven in May 1917 with a message of prayer and peace. You asked the children if they would be willing to offer themselves to God and bear all the sufferings he sent them, as an act of reparation for the conversion of sinners. May we too make such an offering, and accept that, like the children, this may well involve us in suffering, but that the grace of God will also be our comfort.

Now make your petition to Our Lady of Fatima
Our Father, Hail Mary, Glory be…

Day 5

Our Lady of the Rosary, you came from heaven in June 1917 to ask the children to pray the Rosary every day to bring peace to the world. You also asked that devotion to your Immaculate Heart be spread throughout the world, and promised salvation to all who embrace this devotion. Through your intercession may we, too, have the grace to pray the Rosary every day and to embrace this devotion to you, confident that whatever we have to suffer in life, you will never forsake us, in the knowledge that your Immaculate Heart will be our refuge and the way that will lead us to God.

Now make your petition to Our Lady of Fatima
Our Father, Hail Mary, Glory be…

Day 6

Our Lady of the Rosary, you came from heaven in July 1917 to ask the children to continue to pray the Rosary every day to bring peace to the world. You also asked them to sacrifice themselves for sinners, and say many times, especially when they made some sacrifice: "O Jesus, it is for love of you, for the conversion of sinners, and in reparation for the sins committed against the Immaculate Heart of Mary." May we too have the grace to make such sacrifices, both for ourselves and for those in danger of going to hell.

Now make your petition to Our Lady of Fatima
Our Father, Hail Mary, Glory be…

Day 7

Our Lady of the Rosary, you came from heaven in August 1917, and urged the children to continue to say the Rosary every day, and also asked them to "pray, pray very much and make sacrifices for sinners, for many souls go to hell because there are none to sacrifice themselves and to pray for them." May we too have the grace to pray and make sacrifices for ourselves, our families and friends, and the Church and the world.

Now make your petition to Our Lady of Fatima
Our Father, Hail Mary, Glory be…

Day 8

Our Lady of the Rosary, you came from heaven in September 1917 and once more urged the children to pray the Rosary daily. You also told them that God was pleased with their sacrifices. May we, too, have the grace to pray and make sacrifices for the love of God and in reparation for the sins against your Immaculate Heart. You promised the children, too, that you would cure the sick; give us compassion for those who are suffering sickness, and a great faith in your power to heal.

Now make your petition to Our Lady of Fatima
Our Father, Hail Mary, Glory be…

Day 9

Our Lady of the Rosary, you came from heaven in October 1917, asking that a chapel be built in your honour at the Cova da Iria. May we always have the grace to honour you, to pray the Rosary daily, and to pray to you as Our Lady of the Rosary of Fatima. Above all, may we have the grace to take your final words at Fatima to heart: "Do not offend the Lord our God any more, because he is already so much offended."

Now make your petition to Our Lady of Fatima
Our Father, Hail Mary, Glory be…

Fatima and Immaculate Heart Litanies

Litany of Our Lady of Fatima

Our Lady of Fatima, *pray for our dear country.*

Our Lady of Fatima, *sanctify our clergy.*

Our Lady of Fatima, *make our Catholics more fervent.*

Our Lady of Fatima, *guide and inspire those who govern us.*

Our Lady of Fatima, *cure the sick who confide in thee.*

Our Lady of Fatima, *console the sorrowful who trust in thee.*

Our Lady of Fatima, *help those who invoke thine aid.*

Our Lady of Fatima, *deliver us from all dangers.*

Our Lady of Fatima, *help us to resist temptation.*

Our Lady of Fatima, *obtain for us all that we lovingly ask of thee.*

Our Lady of Fatima, *help those who are dear to us.*

Our Lady of Fatima, *bring back to the right road our erring brothers.*

Our Lady of Fatima, *give us back our ancient fervour.*

Our Lady of Fatima, *obtain for us pardon of our manifold sins and offences.*

Our Lady of Fatima, *bring all men to the feet of thy Divine Child.*

Our Lady of Fatima, *obtain peace for the world.*

O Mary conceived without sin, *pray for us who have recourse to thee.*
Immaculate Heart of Mary, *pray for us now and at the hour of our death. Amen.*

Let us pray:
O God of infinite goodness and mercy, fill our hearts with a great confidence in thy dear Mother, whom we invoke under the title of Our Lady of the Rosary and Our Lady of Fatima, and grant us by her powerful intercession all the graces, spiritual and temporal, which we need.
Through Christ Our Lord.
Amen.

Taken from *https://www.ewtn.com/Devotionals/Litanies/fatima.htm*

Litany of Blessed Francisco and Jacinta

Lord, have mercy on us, *Lord, have mercy on us.*
Christ, have mercy on us, *Christ, have mercy on us.*
Lord, have mercy on us, *Lord, have mercy on us.*

God the Father, Creator of the world, *have mercy on us.*
God the Son, Redeemer of mankind, *have mercy on us.*
God the Holy Spirit, perfection of those who are chosen, *have mercy on us.*
Holy Trinity, one God, *have mercy on us.*

Holy Mary, Mother of God, *pray for us.*
Our Lady of the Rosary, *pray for us.*
Immaculate heart of Mary, *pray for us.*

Francisco and Jacinta, children blessed by God,
pray for us.
Children so dear to the Heart of Our Lady, *pray for us.*
Children so loved by all of us, *pray for us.*

Little shepherds, in admiration of the glories of creation,
pray for us.
Little shepherds, gazing in wonder at the starry sky,
pray for us.
Little shepherds, caressing your furry white lambs,
pray for us.
Little shepherds, with your clear innocent gaze,
pray for us.
Little shepherds, with your angelic smile, *pray for us.*
Little shepherds, with your pure soul, *pray for us.*

Hearts enchanted by beauty, *pray for us.*
Hearts yearning for truth, *pray for us.*
Hearts overflowing with love, *pray for us.*
Amazing wonders of prayer, *pray for us.*
Wells brimming over with sacrifices, *pray for us.*
Children totally committed and ready for martyrdom,
pray for us.

Francisco, seeker of peace and contemplation, *pray for us.*
You who would console God, *pray for us.*
You who died smiling, *pray for us.*

Jacinta, faithful helpmate of the Holy Father, *pray for us.*
You, the apostle of the Immaculate Heart of Mary,
pray for us.
You, the friend of sinners, *pray for us.*

You two, who enjoyed the company of angels, *pray for us.*
Confidantes of Our Lady, *pray for us.*
Living witnesses of her message, *pray for us.*
You who loved God so deeply, *pray for us.*
Watchers beside the hidden Jesus, *pray for us.*
Adorers of the most Blessed Trinity, *pray for us.*
Stars of light for all human beings, *pray for us.*
Burning bushes of the Most High, *pray for us.*
Flames of love for all eternity, *pray for us.*

Lamb of God, who take away the sins of the world,
forgive us, O Lord.
Lamb of God, who take away the sins of the world,
hear us, O Lord.
Lamb of God, who take away the sins of the world,
have mercy on us.

Let us pray:
O God who granted to our two little shepherds the grace to
become little burning bushes on fire with love for the Holy
Father and for sinners, and burning with love for Our Lady
and the "hidden" Jesus, grant that we, too, may be other
Franciscos and other Jacintas, so that we, too, may burn

with the same love and, with them, all meet together again in heaven around Our Lady in adoration of the Blessed Trinity. Through Jesus Christ.
Amen.

Litany of the Immaculate Heart of Mary
by Blessed John Henry Newman

Lord, have mercy, *Lord, have mercy.*
Christ, have mercy, *Christ, have mercy.*
Lord, have mercy, *Lord, have mercy.*
Christ, hear us, *Christ, graciously hear us.*

God the Father of Heaven, *have mercy on us.*
God the Son, Redeemer of the world, *have mercy on us.*
God the Holy Spirit, *have mercy on us.*
Holy Trinity, one God, *have mercy on us.*

Heart of Mary, *pray for us.*
Heart of Mary, after God's own Heart, *pray for us.*
Heart of Mary, in union with the Heart of Jesus, *pray for us.*
Heart of Mary, vessel of the Holy Spirit, *pray for us.*
Heart of Mary, shrine of the Trinity, *pray for us.*
Heart of Mary, home of the Word, *pray for us.*
Heart of Mary, immaculate in your creation, *pray for us.*
Heart of Mary, flooded with grace, *pray for us.*
Heart of Mary, blessed of all hearts, *pray for us.*
Heart of Mary, throne of glory, *pray for us.*
Heart of Mary, abyss of humbleness, *pray for us.*

Heart of Mary, victim of love, *pray for us.*
Heart of Mary, nailed to the cross, *pray for us.*
Heart of Mary, comfort of the sad, *pray for us.*
Heart of Mary, refuge of the sinner, *pray for us.*
Heart of Mary, hope of the dying, *pray for us.*
Heart of Mary, seat of mercy, *pray for us.*

Lamb of God, who take away the sins of the world,
spare us, O Lord.
Lamb of God, who take away the sins of the world,
graciously hear us, O Lord.
Lamb of God, who take away the sins of the world,
have mercy on us.

Christ, hear us, *Christ, graciously hear us.*
Lord, have mercy, *Lord, have mercy.*
Christ, have mercy, *Christ, have mercy.*
Lord, have mercy, *Lord, have mercy.*

V. Immaculate Mary, meek and humble of heart.
R. *Conform our hearts to the Heart of Jesus.*

Let us pray:
O most merciful God, who for the salvation of sinners
and the refuge of the wretched, has made the Immaculate
Heart of Mary most like in tenderness and pity to the Heart
of Jesus, grant that we, who now commemorate her most
sweet and loving heart, may by her merits and intercession,
ever live in the fellowship of the hearts of both Mother and
Son, through the same Christ Our Lord. *Amen.*

Fatima Hymns

Fatima Ave

The thirteenth of May
In the Cova da Iria
Appeared, oh so brilliant,
The Virgin Maria.

Refrain
Ave, Ave, Ave Maria (2)

The Virgin Maria
Encircled with light,
Our own dearest Mother
And heaven's delight. *R/.*

To three little shepherds
Our Lady appeared.
The light of her grace
To her Son souls endeared. *R/.*

With war and its evils
The whole world was seething
And countless of thousands
Were mourning and weeping. *R/.*

To save all poor souls
Who had wandered astray,
With sweet words of comfort
She asked us to pray. *R/.*

By honouring Mary
And loving her Son,
The peace of the world
Will most surely be won. *R/.*

Our Lady of Fatima

O come to the throne of grace,
O come to the heart most pure,
To Mary our hope of life,
In whom salvation is sure.

Refrain
Our Lady of Fatima, hail,
Immaculate Mother of Grace,
Oh pray for us, help us today,
Thou hope of the human race.

Immaculate Heart, we kneel,
To consecrate all to thee,
The present, its pain and joy,
The future, all it may be. *R/.*

The sun at thy royal word,
Spun around like a splendid toy,
The rose-petals showering down,
Proclaimed thee cause of our joy. *R/.*

O Virgin of the Rosary

O Virgin of the Rosary,
Of Fatima, dear Lady,
O dearest Queen of Heaven,
To save you're ever ready.
O Virgin of the Rosary,
Of Fatima, dear lady,
As now we leave your sanctuary,
Once more we kneel before thee.

Refrain:
Just one more final prayer
As we leave, oh Mother dear,
May our hearts ever ring,
With the words that we sing:
Oh, Fatima, farewell, Mother dear, farewell,
Oh Fatima, farewell, Mother dear, farewell.

Before we leave, oh Mother,
Oh hear our prayer of sorrow,
And save us from all danger
Today, tonight, tomorrow.

Before we leave, oh Mother,
Have mercy on our sorrow
And ever be our guardian,
Today, tonight, tomorrow. *R/.*

Oh Mother, as we leave you,
The tears to our eyes are springing,
But still our hearts with happiness,
Your love, your praise, are singing.
Oh Mother, as we leave you
Our eyes with tears are dimming,
But though we weep at parting,
Our souls with love are brimming. *R/.*